Title

The Future of Real Estate: Beyond 2030

By Yaswanth (Yeshwanth) Vepachadu

Copyright

© 2024 Yaswanth (Yeshwanth) Vepachadu. All rights reserved.

Title: *The Future of Real Estate: Innovative Models for Sustainable Living, Investment, and Community Building*

Author: Yaswanth Vepachadu

All rights reserved. No part of this publication may be reproduced, distributed, or transmitted in any form or by any means, including photocopying, recording, or other electronic or mechanical methods, without the prior written permission of the author, except in the case of brief quotations embodied in critical reviews and certain other non-commercial uses permitted by copyright law. For permission requests, write to the publisher at the address below.

Email: yaswanth.vepachadu@gmail.com

Disclaimer

The information presented in this book is for informational purposes only and is not intended as investment advice. Readers should conduct their own research and consult with a financial advisor before making any investment decisions. The author and publisher disclaim any liability for any damages or losses incurred by readers as a result of their use of the information presented in this book.

About the Author

Yaswanth Vepachadu is a visionary entrepreneur, author, and thought leader with extensive experience in **real estate innovation, technology, and sustainable development**. Over the years, Yaswanth has been at the forefront of integrating **cutting-edge technologies** like AI, quantum computing, and blockchain into real estate, creating transformative models that are changing the way we think about property ownership, investment, and community living.

Yaswanth is passionate about **regenerative living**, **sustainability**, and the potential of real estate to create meaningful social and environmental impact. His work focuses on merging the best of technology, community, and sustainability to create thriving environments where people and the planet coexist in harmony. He has successfully launched and scaled multiple businesses in the real estate and tech sectors, each aimed at pushing the boundaries of what is possible and exploring new ways to innovate and thrive.

In addition to his business ventures, Yaswanth is an avid writer and educator, committed to sharing his knowledge and inspiring others to reimagine the future of real estate. He believes in the power of **bold ideas** and **collaborative communities** to drive positive change and is dedicated to empowering individuals to take part in building a more inclusive, connected, and sustainable world.

Connect with Yaswanth Vepachadu:
LinkedIn: https://www.linkedin.com/in/yvepachadu/

Table of Contents

Copyright 2
Disclaimer 3
About the Author 4
Preface 6
Introduction: 8
Chapter 1: Meta-Physical Properties 10
Chapter 2: Nomadic Property Trusts 15
Chapter 3: Regenerative Real Estate 21
Chapter 4: Autonomous Property Hubs 27
Chapter 5: Hyper-Modular Communities 34
Chapter 6: Geo-Flex Investment Tokens 41
Chapter 7: Mindful Escapes 47
Chapter 8: Solar Village Co-Investments 54
Chapter 9: Space-Shared Real Estate 60
Chapter 10: Gamified Living Estates 67
Chapter 11: Quantum AI-Based Property Flip Fund 74
Chapter 12: Impact Pods for Regenerative Living 80
Final Summary: A Vision for the Future of Real Estate 86

Preface

The world is changing faster than ever before. Technology is not only altering the way we communicate, work, and travel, but also fundamentally reshaping our understanding of value, ownership, and community. In this ever-evolving landscape, real estate—one of humanity's oldest and most tangible assets—stands on the brink of a monumental transformation. This book is an invitation to explore how the future of real estate will look in 2030 and beyond, as we push past traditional boundaries and embrace new opportunities for innovation, investment, and impact.

Real estate has always been about location, but tomorrow it will be about **mobility, flexibility, and imagination.** The generations coming of age today, from Millennials to Gen Z to Gen Alpha, are looking for more than just a roof over their heads. They value **experiences, sustainability, and community**—and their expectations are reshaping the property landscape. To these generations, ownership is not just a matter of physical possession, but a gateway to opportunity, freedom, and a shared purpose. They seek properties that are integrated with technology, aligned with environmental goals, and capable of evolving with the people who use them.

The ideas in this book are ambitious. They are disruptive. They are, in many ways, a glimpse into a future where the concept of property goes beyond what we see today—encompassing **digital realms, regenerative efforts, autonomous living, and even space exploration.** From investing in virtual-physical hybrid properties to owning a piece of orbital villas for space tourists, this book will explore visionary concepts designed to inspire and challenge your thinking.

The future of real estate is about breaking free from the constraints of traditional ownership and embracing a new model where properties can move, grow, and change along with the people they serve. This book invites you to think beyond the ordinary, to explore concepts that are not only feasible but, in some cases, already beginning to take shape. The goal is to redefine real estate as an active, evolving part of people's lives—integrated with the way we live, work, and experience the world.

Whether you are an investor, a futurist, an entrepreneur, or simply someone with a curiosity for the future, this book will take you on a journey to uncover what real estate could become. Together, we will look at **fifteen groundbreaking models** that push the limits of imagination and technology. The future is closer than you think, and the opportunities are endless. Let's explore how we can reimagine real estate to shape a better, more connected, and sustainable world.

Introduction:

The concept of real estate as we know it is evolving. The way we live, work, and play is undergoing dramatic transformation, driven by technology, changing values, and shifting global dynamics. What if real estate was no longer about static assets, but instead became a fluid part of our everyday experiences? What if properties adapted to the evolving needs of people, prioritized sustainability, and embraced the possibilities of both the physical and digital realms?

The world of 2030 and beyond will be characterized by unprecedented advancements in technology, shifts in economic and environmental priorities, and new approaches to how we see our homes and investments. Generations coming of age during this time—Millennials, Gen Z, and even Gen Alpha—view property ownership in a completely different way compared to past generations. For them, value is not solely about possession; it's about access, experiences, flexibility, and impact. They prioritize mobility over permanence, community over isolation, and shared purpose over solitary ownership.

In this new world, real estate will transcend the traditional notions of buying, renting, and leasing. It will blend with **technology, sustainability, and community** to become an integral part of people's evolving lifestyles. Properties will no longer be fixed and unchanging; instead, they will adapt, evolve, and align with the shifting needs and desires of their occupants. Real estate will become a service, a community, a regenerative force, and even an adventure.

This book explores **fifteen visionary models** that break away from convention. We'll dive into **Meta-Physical Properties** that exist both in reality and in the digital metaverse, **Nomadic Property**

Trusts that redefine mobility by giving owners access to homes around the globe, and **Regenerative Real Estate** that aims to restore ecosystems rather than just occupy space. From **AI-driven autonomous communities** to **solar-powered villages**, to the bold concept of owning real estate in **space**, this book will show you what's possible when we dare to reimagine the boundaries of real estate.

Our journey begins with the recognition that the world is moving fast, and the real estate industry must move with it. The ideas presented here may seem ambitious—even fantastical—but they are built on trends already taking shape today. With advancements in **quantum computing, artificial intelligence, the metaverse, sustainability**, and **space exploration**, the next decade will bring opportunities to invest, experience, and live in ways that we are only beginning to understand.

In a time where **flexibility, community, and experience** are becoming the cornerstones of our lives, real estate must evolve to meet these needs. This book is an invitation to dream big, think differently, and consider the possibilities that lie ahead. The goal is not just to predict the future but to shape it—to be at the forefront of a revolution that will redefine what property means to us.

Welcome to the future of real estate. Let's begin.

Chapter 1: Meta-Physical Properties

Real Estate in a Virtual-Physical Hybrid World

Imagine investing in a property that doesn't just exist in one place or one reality, but spans both the physical and virtual worlds. Welcome to the era of **Meta-Physical Properties**—an idea where bricks and mortar meet bits and pixels, creating a new asset class that bridges tangible real estate with digital spaces in the metaverse.

Picture a downtown high-rise, physically situated in a bustling urban center. Now, imagine a digital twin of this same building existing in the metaverse—a sprawling virtual city where people socialize, work, and entertain themselves. This building is accessible not only to real-world tenants but also to avatars in a vibrant, ever-evolving digital universe. **Meta-Physical Properties** are revolutionizing the notion of ownership, allowing investors to tap into two distinct yet interconnected revenue streams.

The Birth of Meta-Physical Properties

In today's world, we already see the rise of virtual land, with platforms like **Decentraland** and **The Sandbox** gaining immense popularity. But by 2030, the concept of blending the **physical with the digital** will take on new heights. Imagine attending a meeting in your virtual office that's a mirror image of your actual physical workspace, or hosting events where attendees can experience your property either physically or digitally—depending on where they are in the world. This hybrid real estate model isn't just a vision of the future—it's becoming a reality.

Meta-Physical Properties are built on the concept of **digital twins**—exact virtual replicas of physical structures that exist simultaneously in both realities. These digital twins will be designed to offer experiences that go beyond what physical space can provide. Want to see your property in a different design style? In the metaverse, you can change the appearance of your virtual property with a click. Want to host an international art exhibit in your office lobby? The virtual twin will allow for an art experience that people from across the globe can attend without stepping outside their homes.

Dual Revenue Streams: Real and Virtual

One of the most intriguing aspects of Meta-Physical Properties is the ability to **generate income from both realms**. Physical tenants might occupy the building, paying traditional rent. Meanwhile, in the metaverse, virtual tenants, event organizers, or even digital artists could rent the digital twin for their purposes. The property, therefore, becomes a **dual-income asset**, providing revenue streams that weren't possible before.

Consider a real-world example: A high-end luxury hotel that also exists in the metaverse. Guests can book rooms in either version of the hotel. Someone might want to experience a stay physically, while another guest may wish to enjoy a fully immersive digital experience with enhanced, gamified elements. Investors will benefit from having two properties for the price of one, each catering to different target markets and diversifying their income potential.

Blurring the Lines Between Reality and the Virtual

Meta-Physical Properties challenge our traditional understanding of what is real and what is virtual. In a world increasingly comfortable with digital environments—from online gaming to virtual workspaces—people will no longer draw a hard line between the digital and the physical. For many, especially **Gen Z** and **Gen Alpha**, a virtual meeting in a metaverse version of a conference room will feel as natural as an in-person meeting.

This merging of realities opens the door to limitless possibilities for **design, interaction, and revenue creation**. Imagine owning a high-rise with a rooftop garden in the physical world. In its digital twin, you can take it up a notch—expanding that garden into a sprawling forest, adding a sky bridge that connects to other properties, or even creating floating rooms above the garden that defy the limitations of physics. The beauty of Meta-Physical Properties is that they **enhance the real-world experience** while also delivering **unique digital experiences** that break the boundaries of traditional architecture and design.

Access, Exclusivity, and Community

Ownership of Meta-Physical Properties will also grant unique forms of **access and exclusivity**. Imagine holding a **virtual membership pass** to a luxury apartment complex that not only allows you to visit the physical property whenever you want but also provides access to exclusive virtual experiences—concerts, galas, or networking events hosted in the metaverse version of the property. These experiences can build a community that transcends physical boundaries, making Meta-Physical Properties particularly appealing to **investors who value both financial returns and unique engagement opportunities**.

Communities built around Meta-Physical Properties will have the potential to create **hybrid neighborhoods** where people socialize, collaborate, and engage in events—both physically and virtually. Imagine walking into a digital art gallery in the metaverse and simultaneously being able to connect with residents of the real building who are experiencing the gallery physically. The Meta-Physical model fosters a sense of belonging that surpasses the limitations of location and geography.

The Future of Property Management

Managing a Meta-Physical Property will require a new skill set. Property managers will not only deal with maintenance and tenant relationships in the physical world but also oversee the **digital operations**—like optimizing the use of virtual spaces, ensuring that digital tenants or users have a seamless experience, and even upgrading the virtual design to attract more visitors.

Investors in these properties will need to partner with both **traditional property management firms** and **metaverse architects**—designers who specialize in creating compelling virtual experiences. This opens up a new professional landscape, with job roles and careers that currently don't exist but are poised to become highly sought after.

Why Meta-Physical Properties Matter

Meta-Physical Properties offer a compelling value proposition in an increasingly digital world. They allow investors to **diversify their income streams**, hedge against traditional market risks, and cater to a growing demographic that values digital experiences. As more people spend time in virtual spaces—whether for work, entertainment, or socializing—the demand for Meta-Physical spaces will only increase.

Moreover, Meta-Physical Properties bring **sustainability** into the equation. By hosting virtual events and experiences that would otherwise require physical infrastructure, we can reduce our carbon footprint while still offering engaging interactions. Imagine hosting a global conference in a digital twin instead of flying thousands of attendees to a physical location—saving emissions while still providing an immersive experience.

A Gateway to Limitless Possibilities

The true power of Meta-Physical Properties lies in their **flexibility and scalability**. Unlike traditional real estate, which is limited by physical constraints, Meta-Physical Properties can be **expanded, upgraded, and adapted** at will. Want to add a new wing to your virtual office? It's just a few clicks away. Want to enhance the aesthetics of your property with futuristic elements? The possibilities are limited only by imagination.

Meta-physical properties represent a new frontier where **ownership, creativity, and technology intersect**. They offer a glimpse into a future where the walls between our physical and virtual lives dissolve, and where real estate evolves from static brick and mortar into a dynamic, multi-dimensional experience.

By investing in Meta-Physical Properties, you're not just buying a piece of land or a building—you're investing in a vision of the future where real estate is **alive, adaptive, and boundaryless**. Welcome to the hybrid world of tomorrow, where the only limit is your imagination.

Key Features: Digital twins, dual revenue streams, virtual and physical stay options.

Chapter 2: Nomadic Property Trusts

Redefining Real Estate Mobility

Imagine a world where your home isn't defined by a single address, where your investment in property doesn't tie you down but sets you free. A world where your real estate portfolio lets you chase the sun, enjoy endless summers, and immerse yourself in cultures across the globe—all without the hassle of buying, selling, or moving your belongings. Welcome to the future of real estate—**Nomadic Property Trusts**.

Nomadic Property Trusts are the answer to an increasingly mobile generation that values **experiences over ownership** and **freedom over permanence**. They represent a paradigm shift in property investment, enabling investors to own a stake in properties across multiple destinations, enjoy flexible stays, and earn income from high-demand tourist locations. By redefining what it means to "own" property, Nomadic Property Trusts offer a lifestyle of exploration and financial return, all wrapped into one innovative package.

The Birth of Nomadic Living

The traditional concept of homeownership has long been associated with stability—roots in the ground, a fixed address, a place to call your own. But the world is changing, and so is the mindset of new generations. **Millennials and Gen Z** are less interested in settling down and more interested in collecting experiences. The rise of remote work, the gig economy, and digital entrepreneurship has given birth to a new lifestyle—one that doesn't fit neatly into the confines of a single location.

Imagine a world where your "home" isn't limited to a single city or even a single country. Instead, your home is a **network of properties**—a beach villa in Bali, a loft in New York City, a cabin in the Swiss Alps. With Nomadic Property Trusts, investors can own a share of properties in diverse locations and experience them firsthand. This is not just real estate; it's a **passport to a global lifestyle**.

How Nomadic Property Trusts Work

Nomadic Property Trusts (NPTs) operate similarly to Real Estate Investment Trusts (REITs), but with a crucial twist—**mobility and access**. Investors pool their resources to buy and manage a collection of properties across different countries. The properties are chosen based on their appeal as both vacation rentals and temporary residences, ensuring high demand and steady income. But unlike traditional REITs, which are purely about generating financial returns, NPTs come with an **experiential dividend**.

As an investor in a Nomadic Property Trust, you don't just earn returns from rental income—you also gain **access to the properties**. Imagine spending three months working remotely from a beachfront apartment in Costa Rica, then moving to a cozy cottage in Tuscany for the summer. Investors receive **flexible stay credits** that allow them to use the properties within the trust, turning their investment into a living, breathing experience.

Freedom to Explore Without the Hassle

One of the biggest barriers to a nomadic lifestyle is the hassle of logistics—finding a place to live, dealing with leases, navigating foreign property markets, and managing upkeep. Nomadic Property Trusts eliminate these hurdles by providing a seamless experience. All properties within the trust are **professionally**

managed, ensuring they are well-maintained and ready for use whenever you decide to visit.

No more worrying about property maintenance, utility bills, or lease agreements. With NPTs, you have the freedom to **explore the world on your terms**, with the security of knowing that wherever you go, a home awaits you—fully furnished, managed, and ready to welcome you. It's about having the **freedom to roam** while still enjoying the comforts of home.

The Rise of the Global Citizen

Nomadic Property Trusts are tailor-made for the new generation of **global citizens**. These are individuals who see the world as their playground, who feel just as comfortable in a café in Paris as they do at a night market in Bangkok. For these people, the concept of "home" is not tied to a specific place—it's tied to a feeling of belonging, of community, and of being where they want to be at any given moment.

By investing in an NPT, you become part of a **global community** of like-minded individuals who value exploration and freedom. Trust members can connect through exclusive events, shared experiences, and meetups at the various properties. Imagine spending a week at a villa in Bali and meeting other investors who share your passion for travel and adventure. Nomadic Property Trusts create a network that is as much about **community** as it is about investment.

Earning While You Roam

One of the most attractive aspects of Nomadic Property Trusts is the ability to **earn passive income** while embracing a nomadic lifestyle. The properties within the trust are rented out when they are not being used by investors, generating rental income that is distributed among the trust members. This means that even as you enjoy the perks of staying in beautiful locations around the world, your investment is working for you.

Properties are strategically selected based on their rental potential, focusing on high-demand locations that attract tourists, digital nomads, and seasonal visitors. From bustling urban centers to serene countryside retreats, the properties are chosen to ensure a **steady stream of rental income**, maximizing returns for investors. It's about turning the dream of a nomadic lifestyle into a **profitable reality**.

Flexible Stay Credits: Live Where You Want, When You Want

At the heart of Nomadic Property Trusts is the concept of **Flexible Stay Credits**. As an investor, you earn credits that can be used to stay at any of the trust's properties. The more you invest, the more credits you receive, allowing you to tailor your experience to your preferences. Want to spend the winter months soaking up the sun in a Mediterranean villa? Use your credits. Prefer to split your time between a mountain cabin and a city loft? The choice is yours.

This flexibility is what sets NPTs apart from traditional real estate investments. It's not just about financial returns—it's about having the **freedom to design your life**, to choose where you want to be and when. Whether you're a digital nomad looking for new places to work remotely, a retiree seeking adventure, or a family wanting to explore different cultures, Flexible Stay Credits make it possible to **live life on your own terms**.

Sustainable, Smart, and Community-Oriented

Nomadic Property Trusts are also paving the way for **sustainable travel**. The properties within the trust are designed with sustainability in mind—using renewable energy, eco-friendly construction materials, and smart technology to minimize their environmental impact. By sharing properties among multiple investors, NPTs also promote a more efficient use of resources, reducing the need for individual ownership of vacation homes that often sit empty for most of the year.

In addition, the properties are equipped with **smart home technologies** that make remote management easy and efficient. Imagine controlling the thermostat of your cabin in Norway from your smartphone while sitting on a beach in Thailand. Smart technology ensures that the properties are not only comfortable and convenient but also energy-efficient, contributing to a **greener future**.

Nomadic Property Trusts are about more than just owning a piece of real estate—they are about **creating a lifestyle** that is rich in experiences, sustainable, and community-driven. By investing in an NPT, you're not just buying into property; you're buying into a movement that prioritizes **freedom, sustainability, and connection**.

A New Definition of Home

The idea of "home" is evolving. For many, home is no longer a static place where you put down roots and stay for decades. Instead, it's a feeling—a sense of comfort, belonging, and adventure. Nomadic Property Trusts embody this new definition of home. They provide the freedom to move, to explore, and to experience the world without sacrificing the comfort and security that come with having a place to call your own.

With Nomadic Property Trusts, your investment is not just in real estate—it's in **your future, your freedom, and your ability to live life on your own terms**. It's about breaking free from the limitations of traditional property ownership and embracing a world where your home is wherever you want it to be.

Key Features: Shared property ownership, seasonal location switching, income from high-demand areas, Flexible Stay Credits, community events, sustainable living.

Nomadic Property Trusts are more than an investment—they are an invitation to explore, to connect, and to redefine what it means to truly feel at home in the world. It's time to let go of the notion that you need to be tied to one place to find stability. The future is about **mobility, community, and endless exploration**. Welcome to a new way to own property. Welcome to **Nomadic Property Trusts**.

Chapter 3: Regenerative Real Estate

. Healing the Planet Through Property Investment

Imagine a future where owning property doesn't just provide financial returns but actively contributes to healing the planet. Welcome to the concept of **Regenerative Real Estate**—a revolutionary approach that goes beyond sustainability, aiming to restore and rejuvenate ecosystems while providing value to investors. Regenerative Real Estate transforms property investment into an opportunity to **give back to the Earth** rather than simply extracting resources from it.

In a world grappling with climate change, biodiversity loss, and environmental degradation, people are increasingly looking for ways to invest in the planet's future. Regenerative Real Estate is the answer for investors who want to align their financial interests with a larger purpose—**restoring natural habitats, enhancing biodiversity, and making a positive environmental impact**. This chapter will explore how properties can be transformed into thriving ecosystems that generate financial, social, and ecological returns.

The Shift From Sustainable to Regenerative

For years, the term **sustainability** has dominated conversations about the environment and the future of real estate. But sustainability, at its core, is about **maintaining** the status quo—about ensuring that we do not cause further damage. **Regenerative Real Estate** takes it a step further. It's not just about doing less harm; it's about actively doing good—about restoring ecosystems, enhancing natural habitats, and creating environments where both nature and people can thrive.

Imagine a property that doesn't just minimize its carbon footprint but **actively captures carbon**, purifies water, and nurtures local wildlife. Picture a residential development where every home contributes to regenerating the surrounding land—turning barren fields into lush, vibrant ecosystems. Regenerative Real Estate is about embracing the **circular nature of life** and recognizing that human prosperity is intrinsically linked to the health of our planet.

Bringing Nature Back to Real Estate

In Regenerative Real Estate, every property is seen as an **ecosystem**—a living, breathing part of the natural world that can either degrade or regenerate its environment. By adopting regenerative practices, we can turn properties into **biodiversity hotspots**, with gardens that attract pollinators, wetlands that purify water, and forests that provide habitat for birds and small animals. Investors in these properties aren't just buying land; they're investing in **natural capital**—the trees, plants, soil, and water that make life possible.

Consider a residential community built on a degraded plot of land. Instead of leveling the land and building cookie-cutter homes, imagine a development that works **with the landscape**—planting native trees, creating ponds, and designing homes to blend seamlessly into their environment. The result is a property that is not only beautiful but also **functional**—restoring the land, supporting local wildlife, and offering a healthier living environment for residents.

One real-world example of this concept in action is the **Serenbe Community** in Georgia, USA. Serenbe was developed with the goal of creating a community that respects nature and integrates the built environment with the natural world. The community features **organic farms**, **preserved forests**, and a design that encourages human-nature interaction, resulting in a place that's not just sustainable but regenerative—where nature is restored and people live in harmony with the environment.

Turning Waste into Wealth

Regenerative Real Estate is about more than just planting trees and restoring habitats. It's also about **rethinking waste** and transforming it into a valuable resource. Picture a community where every home is equipped with systems to recycle greywater, compost organic waste, and even generate energy from food scraps. Waste becomes part of a **closed-loop system**, feeding back into the land and helping it to regenerate.

For example, organic waste from homes can be composted and used to enrich the soil, while treated greywater can be used to irrigate community gardens. By turning waste into wealth, Regenerative Real Estate not only minimizes the environmental impact of properties but also contributes to the **long-term health and productivity** of the land.

Economic and Ecological Returns

One of the key features of Regenerative Real Estate is its ability to provide **economic returns** alongside **ecological benefits**. Investors in regenerative properties earn revenue from **eco-tourism, carbon credits, organic produce**, and **sustainable product sales**. Imagine owning a share in a regenerative farm where revenue comes not just from property rentals but also from the sale of organic fruits and vegetables grown on-site, or from hosting eco-retreats for people looking to reconnect with nature.

Carbon credits are another significant revenue stream. Properties that actively sequester carbon—through reforestation, soil regeneration, or other means—can earn carbon credits, which can be sold to companies looking to offset their emissions. This creates an incentive for investors to **restore natural landscapes**, knowing that their efforts will be financially rewarded.

In addition to economic benefits, Regenerative Real Estate offers **social returns**. Communities built around regenerative principles tend to be more connected, with residents who are invested in the health of their environment and in the well-being of their neighbors. These communities often feature shared gardens, natural play areas for children, and spaces for gathering—all designed to foster a deeper connection between people and the natural world.

Healing People Through Regenerative Living

The benefits of Regenerative Real Estate extend beyond the environment to include **human health and well-being**. Studies have shown that being in nature has numerous health benefits, including reducing stress, boosting mood, and improving overall physical health. Regenerative properties are designed to maximize the human-nature connection, providing residents with easy access to natural spaces, clean air, and fresh, organically grown food.

Imagine waking up in a home surrounded by native forests, with a garden full of pollinator-friendly flowers just outside your door. Your morning walk takes you along a winding path through restored wetlands, where you might spot birds, butterflies, and even deer. Living in a regenerative community means being constantly immersed in nature, which leads to a **healthier, happier lifestyle**.

The design of regenerative properties also emphasizes **biophilic architecture**—an approach that seeks to connect building occupants more closely to nature. This might include features like **green roofs**, **natural ventilation**, and large windows that let in natural light and provide views of the surrounding landscape. The result is a built environment that not only reduces stress but also encourages a deeper appreciation for the beauty and complexity of the natural world.

Eco-Tourism: Inviting the World to Experience Regeneration

Regenerative Real Estate also opens the door to **eco-tourism**—inviting people to visit and experience the beauty of regenerative living firsthand. Imagine a network of regenerative properties that double as **eco-retreats**, where guests can participate in activities like organic farming, guided nature walks, and workshops on sustainable living. These retreats provide an additional revenue stream for investors while also spreading the message of regeneration to a broader audience.

Guests at these eco-retreats get to experience what it means to live in harmony with nature. They see firsthand how waste is recycled, how water is conserved, and how the land is nurtured back to health. They leave not only feeling refreshed and inspired but also with a deeper understanding of how regenerative practices can be applied in their own lives. By inviting people to experience regeneration, these properties help to create a ripple effect—spreading **awareness and knowledge** far beyond the boundaries of the property itself.

The Future of Regenerative Communities

The future of real estate lies in its ability to **adapt and respond** to the challenges facing our world, and there is no greater challenge than the health of our planet. Regenerative Real Estate represents a shift from ownership that depletes resources to ownership that **restores and regenerates**. It is about recognizing that the value of property is not just in the land or the buildings, but in the **life it supports**—the plants, animals, and people who call it home.

Communities built around regenerative principles are the **communities of the future**. They are resilient, adaptive, and thriving, designed to meet the needs of both people and the planet. These communities will serve as **models for how we can live in**

harmony with the Earth, offering a blueprint for a more sustainable, equitable, and connected world.

Imagine a world where every home contributes to the health of the planet—where the land we live on is alive, thriving, and filled with biodiversity. Imagine owning a piece of that world, knowing that your investment is not only providing financial returns but also making a positive impact on the Earth. Regenerative Real Estate is about more than property ownership—it's about **healing the planet, building community, and creating a future where people and nature thrive together.**

Key Features: Restorative impact, multiple income streams from nature, carbon credits, eco-tourism, biophilic design, waste-to-wealth systems.

Regenerative Real Estate is a call to action for investors who want to be part of the solution—who want their investments to not only secure their future but also the future of the planet. It's time to reimagine what real estate can be. It's time to invest in a world where **regeneration, not extraction, defines value**. Welcome to Regenerative Real Estate—a movement that's turning property into a force for good.

Chapter 4: Autonomous Property Hubs

AI-Driven, Self-Sustaining Real Estate

Imagine owning a property that essentially takes care of itself. From maintenance and energy management to security and community services, everything is controlled seamlessly by **artificial intelligence**. Welcome to **Autonomous Property Hubs**—a futuristic real estate model where AI takes the wheel, offering an experience that is both effortless and profoundly efficient. This chapter explores how the power of AI can transform properties into self-sustaining, self-optimizing entities that allow owners and residents to enjoy a hassle-free, technologically advanced lifestyle.

In a world increasingly dependent on smart technologies, the concept of autonomous properties represents a bold new chapter in real estate—one where automation, sustainability, and convenience are perfectly intertwined. Picture a property that intelligently manages energy consumption, schedules its own maintenance, and even enhances the overall well-being of its occupants. Autonomous Property Hubs are not only about making life easier; they are about **redefining the relationship between people and the spaces they inhabit**.

The Rise of Autonomous Living

As our lives become more connected through smart devices and intelligent systems, the demand for automated and AI-driven solutions has skyrocketed. Today, we already have **smart homes** that allow us to control lighting, security, and entertainment systems through our phones. But what if entire residential complexes or mixed-use properties could go a step further—**managing themselves without human intervention?**

Autonomous Property Hubs are the answer to this growing demand for intelligent living. These properties use advanced AI algorithms to oversee every aspect of property management, transforming the way people interact with their homes and communities. Imagine a building that knows when it needs repairs, that optimizes energy consumption based on weather forecasts, and that even curates community events based on residents' preferences. These hubs are designed to be **adaptive, efficient, and capable of learning**, constantly evolving to meet the needs of their inhabitants.

AI at the Core of Property Management

At the heart of Autonomous Property Hubs is a sophisticated AI-powered property management system that takes care of day-to-day operations. From **predictive maintenance** to **energy optimization**, the AI is capable of making decisions that enhance the property's efficiency and the residents' quality of life. No more unexpected breakdowns or skyrocketing energy bills—AI anticipates potential issues before they become problems and takes action to prevent them.

For instance, the AI can monitor the building's infrastructure in real time, using sensors to detect wear and tear in key systems like plumbing or electrical wiring. When an issue is detected, the AI automatically schedules a repair before it turns into a costly emergency. By keeping the property in peak condition, Autonomous Property Hubs reduce operational costs and extend the lifespan of building systems—making them **cost-effective investments** for property owners.

Energy management is another crucial aspect where AI shines. Autonomous Property Hubs are designed to be **energy-independent**, using renewable energy sources such as solar panels combined with **smart grids** to ensure efficient energy distribution. AI continuously monitors energy usage and weather patterns to optimize the building's energy consumption, storing excess energy during peak generation times and utilizing it when demand is high. This not only minimizes the environmental footprint of the property but also reduces energy costs, creating a more sustainable and affordable living experience for residents.

A Personalized Living Experience

Autonomous Property Hubs are not just about automation—they are about creating a **personalized, intuitive living experience**. The AI system in each hub learns the preferences of residents, from their preferred room temperature to their daily routines. Imagine coming home after a long day to find your apartment already set to the perfect temperature, with your favorite music playing softly in the background and the lights adjusting to match your mood. The AI knows what you need before you even ask for it.

But the personalization goes beyond individual apartments. Autonomous Property Hubs are designed to foster a sense of **community** by curating experiences that bring people together. The AI analyzes data about residents' interests and hobbies to organize events like yoga classes, movie nights, or communal gardening sessions. The result is a vibrant community where people feel connected—not just to their living space but also to their neighbors.

Off-Grid Living: Self-Sustaining Ecosystems

One of the most exciting aspects of Autonomous Property Hubs is their potential for **off-grid living**. These properties are designed to be self-sustaining ecosystems, capable of generating their own power, managing their own water supply, and even growing their own food. Imagine a residential complex equipped with **vertical gardens** that provide fresh produce for residents, or a water recycling system that reduces overall consumption by treating and reusing greywater.

The integration of renewable energy sources like **solar panels, wind turbines, and geothermal systems** allows these properties to operate independently of the traditional energy grid. Energy storage solutions, such as advanced battery systems, ensure that power is always available—even during periods of low generation. By embracing off-grid technologies, Autonomous Property Hubs offer a level of **resilience and sustainability** that is unmatched by conventional properties.

The goal is to create a living environment that is not only comfortable and convenient but also **environmentally responsible**. By reducing reliance on external resources and minimizing waste, these properties contribute to a healthier planet while providing a higher quality of life for residents. Autonomous Property Hubs are a glimpse into a future where real estate is part of the solution to global challenges like climate change and resource scarcity.

Enhanced Security Through AI

Security is a top priority in any residential community, and Autonomous Property Hubs leverage the power of AI to provide **unmatched safety and peace of mind**. AI-driven security systems monitor the property 24/7, using **facial recognition, motion detection, and behavioral analytics** to identify potential threats and respond in real time. The AI can distinguish between a resident, a visitor, and an intruder, ensuring that only authorized individuals have access to the property.

In addition to physical security, Autonomous Property Hubs are equipped with **cybersecurity measures** to protect residents' data and privacy. As properties become more connected, the risk of cyberattacks increases—but AI ensures that all systems are secure, continuously monitoring for vulnerabilities and implementing safeguards to protect against threats. The result is a living environment where residents can feel safe—both physically and digitally.

The Future of Property Ownership

Autonomous Property Hubs are not just changing the way we live; they are also transforming the concept of **property ownership**. In a world where convenience and flexibility are highly valued, these properties offer a unique value proposition: **effortless ownership**. Property owners do not have to worry about managing tenants, handling maintenance requests, or dealing with energy bills—the AI takes care of it all. This makes Autonomous Property Hubs an attractive option for investors who want to enjoy the benefits of real estate without the typical headaches of property management.

Moreover, these properties are designed to be **scalable**. An Autonomous Property Hub can start as a single residential building and expand into a larger community, with AI systems that integrate seamlessly to manage everything from individual apartments to shared amenities and community services. This scalability makes them suitable for a wide range of applications, from **urban residential complexes** to **rural off-grid retreats**.

Community and Connectivity

At their core, Autonomous Property Hubs are about more than just technology—they are about **connection**. By automating mundane tasks and optimizing property management, these hubs give residents more time to focus on what truly matters: building relationships, pursuing passions, and enjoying life. The AI-driven community features foster a sense of belonging, encouraging residents to come together, share experiences, and create lasting memories.

Imagine living in a community where everything is designed to enhance your well-being. The AI organizes wellness programs, fitness classes, and community dinners—all based on residents' preferences. It can even match residents with similar interests, helping to form friendships and strengthen the community. Autonomous Property Hubs are not just places to live; they are places to **thrive**.

A Vision of Effortless Living

The vision of Autonomous Property Hubs is one of **effortless living**—where residents can enjoy the benefits of advanced technology without being overwhelmed by it. The AI works quietly in the background, ensuring that everything runs smoothly while giving people the freedom to live their lives without worrying about the details. It's about creating a living environment that is **intelligent, adaptive, and responsive** to the needs of its inhabitants.

As technology continues to evolve, the potential for Autonomous Property Hubs will only grow. We can imagine a future where these properties are equipped with **robotic maintenance systems** that can perform repairs autonomously, or where AI-driven **community marketplaces** allow residents to trade goods and services seamlessly. The possibilities are limitless, and the impact on our quality of life will be profound.

Autonomous Property Hubs represent the next frontier in real estate—a frontier where technology, sustainability, and human connection come together to create a living experience that is truly **revolutionary**. By investing in these properties, you are not just buying real estate; you are investing in a vision of the future—one where life is easier, more connected, and more fulfilling.

Key Features: AI management, energy independence, off-grid living, enhanced security, personalized living experience, community-driven events, scalability.

Autonomous Property Hubs are a bold step forward in the evolution of real estate. They offer a glimpse into a world where property ownership is **hassle-free**, where communities are connected and thriving, and where the environment is respected and nurtured. It's time to embrace the power of AI and take real estate into the future—toward a world of **autonomous, self-sustaining living** that enhances every aspect of our lives.

Chapter 5: Hyper-Modular Communities

Living, Reimagined: Dynamic, Movable Property Units

Imagine a neighborhood where your home is not anchored to a single plot of land, but instead, it can move and transform to meet your evolving needs. Welcome to **Hyper-Modular Communities**—a visionary concept that reimagines real estate as a fluid, adaptable ecosystem where homes are designed to be flexible, dynamic, and personalized. In Hyper-Modular Communities, the focus is not just on building houses but on creating an environment that grows, changes, and evolves with the people who live there.

In a world where mobility and adaptability are increasingly valued, Hyper-Modular Communities are paving the way for a new kind of living—one that emphasizes **freedom, creativity, and a deep connection to community**. Picture a residential area where homes are composed of movable modules that can be reconfigured based on your lifestyle, family needs, or even the season. Whether you need extra space for a new family member, want to downsize after the kids move out, or just crave a change of scenery, Hyper-Modular Communities provide the ultimate flexibility.

The Concept of Hyper-Modularity

At its core, **hyper-modularity** is about flexibility and personalization. Homes in Hyper-Modular Communities are built from **modular units** that can be easily added, removed, or rearranged. These modules are designed to fit together like building blocks, allowing residents to customize their homes in real time.

Want to add a new bedroom or a rooftop garden? Simply attach a new module. Looking to create an open space for a special gathering? Rearrange the modules to suit the occasion.

Hyper-Modular Communities are like living **Lego worlds**, where each home is a reflection of its occupant's personality, lifestyle, and dreams. The modular units are constructed off-site and delivered to the community, where they are seamlessly integrated into the existing structure. This process not only makes construction faster and more efficient but also ensures that each home is built to the highest quality standards, using sustainable and environmentally friendly materials.

A Dynamic Living Experience

The beauty of Hyper-Modular Communities lies in their **dynamic nature**. Unlike traditional neighborhoods, which are static and unchanging, these communities are in a constant state of evolution. Homes can grow as families expand, shrink as children move out, or even be relocated to a different part of the community if a change of scenery is desired. This flexibility creates a living experience that is **responsive and adaptable** to the changing needs of its residents.

Imagine a young couple moving into a Hyper-Modular Community. They start with a small, cozy home composed of just a few modules. As their family grows, they add new modules—a nursery, an extra bedroom, a play area. When their children become teenagers and need more space, they expand further, creating private rooms and separate living areas. Years later, when the children move out, the couple can downsize by removing some of the modules, creating a more manageable space that suits their new lifestyle. Hyper-Modular Communities make it possible to have a home that grows and changes **in sync with your life**.

But the adaptability doesn't stop at individual homes. Entire neighborhoods within Hyper-Modular Communities are designed to be **reconfigurable**. Public spaces can be expanded or reduced based on community needs, amenities can be relocated, and even the layout of streets and walkways can be adjusted to create the most efficient and enjoyable living environment. It's a neighborhood that **adapts to the community**, not the other way around.

Community-Centric Design

Hyper-Modular Communities are built with a strong emphasis on **community and connection**. The modular nature of the homes makes it easy to create shared spaces—communal gardens, co-working areas, play zones for children, and outdoor entertainment areas. The layout of the community can be adjusted to foster a sense of togetherness, with homes clustered around central courtyards or arranged to create intimate gathering spots.

Imagine a community where neighbors can decide, collectively, to create a new shared space. Perhaps a group of families wants to create a communal garden where they can grow organic vegetables. They simply pool their resources, bring in the necessary modules, and within weeks, a vibrant garden takes shape—complete with raised beds, a greenhouse, and even a small seating area for gatherings. Hyper-Modular Communities make it easy for residents to **shape their environment** and create spaces that bring people together.

The sense of community is further enhanced by **modular amenities**—shared facilities that can be easily added, upgraded, or relocated based on residents' preferences. Whether it's a gym, a library, a workshop, or even a pop-up café, the amenities in Hyper-Modular Communities are designed to be as flexible and dynamic as the homes themselves. This adaptability ensures that the community is always evolving to meet the changing interests and needs of its residents.

Sustainable and Smart Living

Sustainability is at the heart of Hyper-Modular Communities. The modular units are constructed using **sustainable materials** and designed for **energy efficiency**. Solar panels, rainwater harvesting systems, and green roofs are integrated into the design of each module, making these communities environmentally friendly and **energy self-sufficient**. The modular nature of the homes also means that resources are used efficiently—no more building large homes that sit half-empty for years. Instead, each home is the right size for its occupants, with the ability to grow or shrink as needed.

The communities are also equipped with **smart technology** that makes life easier and more efficient. Imagine a home where each module is equipped with smart sensors that monitor energy usage, optimize lighting and temperature, and even alert you to maintenance needs. The entire community is connected through a **centralized AI system** that manages shared resources, coordinates community activities, and ensures that everything runs smoothly. This integration of smart technology creates a living experience that is **convenient, comfortable, and sustainable**.

Mobility: Homes That Move With You

One of the most groundbreaking features of Hyper-Modular Communities is the ability to **relocate modules**. Imagine falling in love with a different part of the community—perhaps you want to move closer to friends, or you crave a better view of the park. In a Hyper-Modular Community, you can do just that. The modular design allows entire sections of your home to be moved to a new location, giving you the freedom to change your surroundings without having to leave the community.

This mobility also means that homes can be **temporarily relocated** to meet specific needs. For instance, if a community member requires a more accessible living space due to an injury or health condition, modules can be swapped out or reconfigured to create a barrier-free environment. Hyper-Modular Communities are designed to be **inclusive and responsive**, ensuring that every resident's needs are met.

A Vision for the Future of Urban Living

Hyper-Modular Communities represent a bold vision for the future of urban living—one that prioritizes **flexibility, sustainability, and community**. As cities become more crowded and the demand for adaptable housing solutions grows, these communities offer a way to make the most of limited space while providing residents with the freedom to shape their environment.

Imagine urban neighborhoods where every home is unique, where public spaces evolve to reflect the interests of the community, and where the built environment is **alive, constantly changing, and adapting**. Hyper-Modular Communities are about more than just housing—they are about creating a new kind of urban fabric, one that is **collaborative, creative, and deeply connected**.

These communities are particularly well-suited to the needs of a world where **remote work** and **digital nomadism** are becoming more common. In a Hyper-Modular Community, you could have a home base that evolves with you, whether you're working remotely, starting a family, or seeking a quieter space to enjoy retirement. The adaptability of these communities makes them an ideal solution for people at all stages of life, providing the stability of homeownership with the freedom of a more flexible lifestyle.

The Emotional Connection to Space

One of the most compelling aspects of Hyper-Modular Communities is the **emotional connection** they foster between people and their living spaces. In traditional housing, homes are static—once they're built, they don't change. But in a Hyper-Modular Community, your home is an extension of yourself. It changes as you change, grows as you grow, and adapts to meet your evolving needs. This creates a deeper emotional bond between residents and their homes, as each home becomes a **living reflection of its occupants**.

The ability to actively shape your environment—whether by adding new modules, creating shared spaces, or relocating your home—gives residents a sense of **agency** and **ownership** that is often missing in traditional housing. In Hyper-Modular Communities, you are not just a resident; you are an active participant in the creation of your living environment. This sense of empowerment fosters pride, satisfaction, and a genuine connection to the community.

Hyper-Modular Communities: Building the Future Together

Hyper-Modular Communities are more than just a new way to build homes—they are a new way to **think about community, connection, and the relationship between people and their environment**. They offer a vision of a future where housing is not static but dynamic, where communities are not rigid but flexible, and where people have the power to shape their surroundings in meaningful ways.

By investing in Hyper-Modular Communities, you are investing in a **future of adaptability, creativity, and sustainability**. It's a future where housing is designed to be as unique as the people who live in it, where neighborhoods evolve to meet the changing needs of their residents, and where the line between private and communal space is blurred in the best possible way. Welcome to Hyper-Modular Communities—a place where **living is reimagined**, and where the possibilities are truly endless.

Key Features: Reconfigurable units, community growth investments, dynamic value appreciation, mobility of homes, sustainable and smart technology integration, community-centric design.

Hyper-Modular Communities are the embodiment of flexibility and innovation in real estate. They offer a new way of living—one that adapts to your lifestyle, fosters community connections, and embraces the ever-changing nature of life. It's time to leave behind the limitations of static housing and step into a world where your home is as **dynamic, creative, and full of potential as you are.**

Chapter 6: Geo-Flex Investment Tokens

Real Estate on the Move—Globally

Imagine owning a piece of the world—a portfolio of properties across multiple countries that can be easily traded and moved at will, all with the simplicity of a token. Welcome to **Geo-Flex Investment Tokens**, the next frontier in real estate investment that transcends borders and redefines the concept of ownership. In a future where mobility is key, Geo-Flex Tokens offer investors the ultimate flex

ibility: the ability to shift their investments across different global locations, capturing market trends, high demand seasons, and the excitement of new opportunities.

Geo-Flex Investment Tokens are designed for a new generation of investors—those who crave diversity, freedom, and a chance to be a part of multiple cities across the globe. This chapter explores how these tokens are transforming real estate into an agile asset, allowing owners to adapt to market dynamics and giving a new meaning to the idea of truly **owning a slice of the world**.

The Concept of Geo-Flex Tokens

Geo-Flex Investment Tokens are digital assets that represent fractional ownership in a curated portfolio of properties across different cities and countries. Unlike traditional real estate investments, where ownership is tied to a single location, Geo-Flex Tokens allow investors to have a **flexible stake in multiple locations**. These tokens can be used to gain exposure to high-demand markets during peak seasons, ensuring that your investment is always working in your favor.

Imagine having an investment that allows you to shift your focus from a beach villa in Bali during the holiday season to a bustling urban apartment in Tokyo during the cherry blossom festival. Geo-Flex Tokens provide investors with **agility and adaptability**—allowing them to capitalize on trends, seasonality, and emerging opportunities in a way that traditional property ownership cannot.

Global Mobility: An Investment That Moves With You

The unique advantage of Geo-Flex Tokens lies in their ability to move with the market. Unlike traditional real estate investments, which can be difficult to liquidate or reposition, Geo-Flex Tokens can be **easily traded or exchanged** within a global marketplace. This means that if one city is experiencing a surge in property value or rental demand, investors can quickly reallocate their tokens to take advantage of these market shifts.

Imagine being able to move your investment from London to Dubai when rental yields are soaring, or from a ski lodge in the Alps to a coastal retreat in Spain during peak summer. Geo-Flex Tokens give investors the power to make **data-driven decisions** and ensure that their real estate portfolio is always aligned with the most lucrative opportunities. This level of **agility** is unheard of in traditional real estate, where buying and selling properties often involves lengthy processes and significant transaction costs.

The tokens are managed through a **blockchain-based platform** that ensures transparency, security, and ease of transfer. This decentralized approach not only makes transactions faster and more secure but also opens up the world of real estate investment to a broader audience. By removing the barriers of location and liquidity, Geo-Flex Tokens are democratizing access to **global property markets**.

Fractional Ownership for the Modern Investor

Geo-Flex Tokens offer **fractional ownership**, making it possible for investors to gain exposure to high-value properties without the need for large capital outlays. Instead of purchasing an entire apartment in New York City or a villa in Santorini, investors can buy tokens that represent a share of these properties. This approach makes real estate investment more accessible, allowing individuals to **diversify their portfolio** across multiple locations without the need for millions of dollars in upfront capital.

For example, an investor could own tokens representing a share of a luxury penthouse in Dubai, a countryside estate in Tuscany, and a trendy loft in Sydney—all through a single investment. The ability to diversify across different geographies and property types reduces risk and provides a **balanced investment strategy** that is resilient to market fluctuations.

Fractional ownership also means that investors can enjoy **income from multiple sources**. Rental income generated by the properties is distributed proportionally to token holders, creating a steady stream of passive income. Whether it's rental yields from a bustling city center during tourist season or the income from a serene countryside retreat, Geo-Flex Tokens ensure that investors are always reaping the benefits of their diversified portfolio.

Seasonal Switching and High-Demand Targeting

One of the most exciting aspects of Geo-Flex Tokens is the ability to **target high-demand seasons**. Properties in the portfolio are strategically chosen to ensure that there is always an opportunity to capture rental income during peak periods. Investors can switch their tokens to properties that are in high demand during specific times of the year—such as a ski resort during winter or a beachfront villa during summer.

Imagine owning a share of a chalet in the French Alps during ski season, then reallocating your tokens to a villa in the Caribbean during the summer holidays. This ability to **seasonally switch investments** allows investors to maximize rental income and ensures that their investment is always working to its full potential. By capitalizing on seasonality, Geo-Flex Tokens offer a level of profitability that static, single-location properties simply cannot match.

Freedom of Experience: Live Where You Invest

Geo-Flex Tokens also come with a unique perk—**the freedom to experience the properties you invest in**. Investors are given the opportunity to stay in the properties they hold tokens for, turning their investment into a lifestyle experience. Imagine spending a week in a luxury apartment in New York City, followed by a month in a peaceful vineyard estate in France, all as part of your investment.

This **experiential aspect** of Geo-Flex Tokens makes them particularly appealing to a new generation of investors who value experiences over material possessions. It's about more than just financial returns—it's about having the freedom to explore the world, to live in different places, and to truly experience the properties you own. Geo-Flex Tokens turn real estate investment into an **adventure**, allowing investors to immerse themselves in the culture, lifestyle, and beauty of different locations around the globe.

A Decentralized Marketplace for Real Estate

Geo-Flex Tokens are traded on a **decentralized marketplace**, where investors can buy, sell, and exchange their tokens with ease. This marketplace operates on blockchain technology, ensuring that every transaction is **secure, transparent, and immutable**. The decentralized nature of the platform means that investors have full control over their tokens, without the need for intermediaries or traditional real estate agents.

The marketplace also provides real-time data on property values, rental yields, and market trends, allowing investors to make **informed decisions** about where to allocate their tokens. By combining the transparency of blockchain with the flexibility of tokenized assets, Geo-Flex Tokens are creating a new standard for real estate investment—one that is **agile, accessible, and inclusive**.

A Portfolio That Adapts to You

In a world where change is the only constant, Geo-Flex Tokens offer a way to ensure that your real estate investments are always **adaptable and resilient**. Whether you're looking to capitalize on emerging markets, diversify your portfolio, or simply enjoy the freedom of experiencing different parts of the world, Geo-Flex Tokens provide the flexibility to do it all. It's an investment that evolves with you, responding to changes in the market and aligning with your personal goals and aspirations.

Imagine being able to shift your investment focus as new opportunities arise—perhaps a booming tech hub in Asia, a growing tourism destination in South America, or a revitalized historic district in Europe. Geo-Flex Tokens allow you to be **agile and responsive**, ensuring that your portfolio is always positioned for growth and profitability. This level of flexibility is what makes Geo-Flex Tokens the ideal investment for a future defined by **mobility, diversity, and opportunity**.

Geo-Flex Tokens: Owning the World, One Slice at a Time

Geo-Flex Investment Tokens represent a revolutionary approach to real estate—one that breaks down borders, embraces flexibility, and redefines what it means to own property. By offering fractional ownership, seasonal switching, and the freedom to experience the properties you invest in, Geo-Flex Tokens are turning real estate into a **dynamic, accessible, and truly global asset**.

Whether you're an experienced investor looking to diversify your portfolio or a digital nomad seeking a way to invest in the places you love, Geo-Flex Tokens provide a way to **own the world, one slice at a time**. It's about more than just financial returns—it's about having the freedom to explore, to adapt, and to live life on your own terms. Welcome to the future of real estate investment—welcome to **Geo-Flex**.

Key Features: Location-switching ownership, dynamic property management, rental optimization, decentralized marketplace, fractional ownership, seasonal investment targeting, experiential benefits.

Geo-Flex Investment Tokens are transforming the way we think about real estate, offering a new level of flexibility, diversity, and freedom. It's time to embrace a world where owning property is no longer limited by borders or burdens—where real estate becomes a **fluid, adaptable, and global experience**. Step into the future of property investment, and let your portfolio move with the world.

Chapter 7: Mindful Escapes

Real Estate & Wellbeing Investment

Imagine a property that isn't just an investment in real estate, but also an investment in your wellbeing—a sanctuary that offers both financial returns and the promise of rest, rejuvenation, and mental clarity. Welcome to **Mindful Escapes**—a revolutionary concept in real estate that combines property investment with the growing desire for **mental health and wellness**. In a world that is increasingly fast-paced, stressful, and disconnected, Mindful Escapes represent an oasis of calm, a place where investors can retreat from the pressures of daily life and find a sense of balance.

Mindful Escapes are properties designed specifically to promote **mental and emotional wellbeing**. They are more than just vacation homes; they are curated experiences that offer holistic wellness, a connection to nature, and a respite from the chaos of the modern world. This chapter will explore how these unique properties are creating value—not just through rental income and property appreciation, but by providing investors with a meaningful, rejuvenating experience.

The Rise of Wellness Real Estate

In recent years, the concept of **wellness** has become a defining element of modern life. As people become more aware of the importance of mental health, they are seeking out spaces that promote relaxation, mindfulness, and personal growth. The rise of wellness retreats, yoga studios, and meditation centers reflects a cultural shift toward **self-care** and **holistic health**. Mindful Escapes take this trend one step further, creating properties that are fully dedicated to enhancing both physical and mental wellbeing.

Mindful Escapes are developed in serene, natural locations—**mountain retreats, lakeside cottages, coastal sanctuaries, and forest hideaways**—where the natural beauty of the surroundings plays a crucial role in promoting relaxation and stress relief. These properties are built with a focus on **sustainable architecture** and **biophilic design**, incorporating natural materials, open spaces, and an abundance of greenery to create an environment that soothes the mind and nourishes the soul.

Properties Designed for Wellbeing

The design of Mindful Escapes is centered around creating a **healing environment**. The architecture is inspired by the principles of **biophilic design**, which emphasizes a strong connection to nature. Large windows bring in natural light and provide stunning views of the surrounding landscape. Open-air spaces, natural materials like wood and stone, and thoughtfully designed gardens all work together to create an environment that promotes relaxation and tranquility.

Each property features **meditation rooms, yoga studios, and wellness facilities** such as saunas, hot tubs, and massage rooms. The interiors are carefully curated to provide a sense of peace, with minimalist decor, calming colors, and natural textures. Mindful Escapes are not just places to stay—they are places to **heal, grow, and reconnect**.

The surrounding landscape is also an integral part of the experience. Imagine waking up to the sound of birdsong, enjoying your morning coffee on a sun-drenched terrace overlooking a peaceful lake, or taking a walk through a forest trail that begins right at your doorstep. Mindful Escapes provide a way for residents and guests to immerse themselves in nature, to leave behind the distractions of modern life, and to find a deeper sense of **balance and harmony**.

A Community of Wellness

Mindful Escapes are not just about individual wellbeing—they are about creating a **community of like-minded individuals** who value health, mindfulness, and connection. These properties often include **communal spaces** where guests can come together for yoga classes, guided meditation sessions, or simply to share a meal. Wellness experts, from yoga instructors to nutritionists, are often on-site to offer personalized guidance and support.

Imagine being part of a community where everyone is there to relax, recharge, and focus on their wellbeing. The sense of connection that comes from shared experiences—whether it's a sunrise yoga session or a cooking class focused on healthy, organic meals—adds an extra layer of meaning to the Mindful Escapes experience. It's about more than just relaxation; it's about creating **lasting relationships** and a supportive community that nurtures mental health and wellbeing.

An Investment in Health and Wealth

Mindful Escapes offer investors a unique value proposition: the ability to earn **rental income** while also having access to a wellness retreat that they can use themselves. These properties are ideal for short-term rentals, attracting guests who are looking for a peaceful getaway, a place to disconnect from technology, and an opportunity to focus on their health. The demand for wellness tourism has been growing rapidly, and Mindful Escapes are perfectly positioned to capitalize on this trend.

For investors, the financial returns come from two main sources: **rental income** and **property appreciation**. The wellness tourism market is booming, with more people seeking out experiences that promote relaxation and personal growth. This makes Mindful

Escapes highly desirable as vacation rentals, ensuring a steady stream of income. Additionally, the unique nature of these properties and their focus on wellness make them valuable assets that are likely to appreciate over time.

But beyond financial returns, Mindful Escapes offer something even more valuable: **access to a sanctuary**. Investors have the opportunity to use these properties themselves, to take a break from their busy lives, and to focus on their own wellbeing. It's an investment that pays dividends in terms of both health and happiness—a way to ensure that the pressures of modern life don't take a toll on your mental health.

The Healing Power of Nature

The natural surroundings of Mindful Escapes play a crucial role in their ability to promote wellbeing. Research has shown that spending time in nature has numerous benefits for mental health—it reduces stress, lowers blood pressure, improves mood, and enhances overall wellbeing. Mindful Escapes are designed to provide **direct access to nature**, making it easy for guests to spend time outdoors, whether it's hiking, swimming, practicing yoga, or simply sitting quietly and enjoying the view.

Each property is designed to create opportunities for **nature immersion**. Trails lead from the doorstep into the surrounding landscape, whether it's a forest, a mountain, or a beach. Outdoor seating areas, meditation decks, and open-air pavilions provide spaces for reflection and relaxation. The goal is to create a seamless connection between the indoor and outdoor spaces, allowing residents and guests to experience the full benefits of being in nature.

Mindful Design: Architecture That Heals

The architecture of Mindful Escapes is not only beautiful but also deeply **intentional**. Every element is designed with the goal of promoting relaxation and reducing stress. The use of natural materials like wood, stone, and clay helps to create a warm, grounding environment. Large windows and open spaces provide **natural light** and fresh air, while indoor gardens and water features bring elements of the natural world inside.

The layout of each property is designed to encourage a **sense of flow**—spaces transition seamlessly from one to the next, creating an experience that is both calming and intuitive. Meditation rooms are placed in quiet corners, away from communal areas, while outdoor spaces are positioned to take advantage of the best views. The design of Mindful Escapes is about more than aesthetics; it's about creating a space that **nurtures the mind, body, and spirit**.

Wellness Retreats and Programs

Mindful Escapes also serve as venues for **wellness retreats and programs**, providing additional income opportunities for investors. These retreats are led by experts in fields such as yoga, meditation, nutrition, and holistic health, offering guests a chance to immerse themselves in a structured program focused on wellbeing. From weekend getaways to week-long immersive experiences, the retreats hosted at Mindful Escapes are designed to provide guests with the tools they need to improve their mental and physical health.

Imagine a week-long retreat focused on **mindfulness and stress reduction**. Guests start each day with guided meditation, followed by yoga and a healthy, organic breakfast. Workshops on topics like nutrition, mental health, and self-care are held throughout the day, along with opportunities for nature walks, journaling, and relaxation. By the end of the retreat, guests leave feeling rejuvenated, equipped with new skills for managing stress, and with a renewed sense of connection to themselves and the world around them.

These wellness retreats not only provide a valuable service to guests but also create a **steady stream of income** for investors. The growing popularity of wellness tourism means that there is a high demand for these kinds of experiences, making Mindful Escapes a profitable investment opportunity.

A Retreat From the Digital World

In today's hyper-connected world, the constant barrage of notifications, emails, and social media can be overwhelming. Mindful Escapes offer a **retreat from the digital world**, providing guests with a chance to **disconnect** from technology and reconnect with themselves. Many of these properties encourage a **digital detox**—no WiFi, no screens, just the sounds of nature and the opportunity to be fully present in the moment.

For many guests, the chance to disconnect is one of the most appealing aspects of Mindful Escapes. It provides a break from the stress and distractions of modern life, allowing guests to experience **true relaxation and mental clarity**. By offering an environment that is free from the demands of technology, Mindful Escapes help guests to find a sense of peace that is increasingly difficult to come by in our connected world.

Mindful Escapes: Investing in Wellbeing

Mindful Escapes represent a new kind of real estate investment—one that offers **financial returns, personal wellbeing, and a meaningful connection to nature**. These properties are designed for those who value both their health and their wealth, providing a way to invest in real estate while also investing in a lifestyle of mindfulness, relaxation, and rejuvenation.

Whether you're an investor looking for a profitable opportunity in the booming wellness market or someone who wants to have a personal sanctuary to escape to, Mindful Escapes offer the perfect balance of **health, wealth, and happiness**. It's about more than just property ownership; it's about owning a place that heals, that nurtures, and that provides a refuge from the demands of modern life. Welcome to Mindful Escapes—where real estate and wellbeing come together in perfect harmony.

Key Features: Wellness-focused design, rental and service revenue, biophilic architecture, community-driven wellness programs, immersive nature experiences, digital detox environments.

Mindful Escapes are a testament to the power of real estate to transform lives—not just by providing financial security but by creating spaces that promote health, happiness, and a deeper connection to the natural world. It's time to invest in a future where **wellbeing is at the heart of property ownership**, where real estate becomes a force for good in the lives of those who experience it.

Chapter 8: Solar Village Co-Investments

Communities Powered by Renewable Energy

Imagine a village where every home, every streetlight, every community center is powered by the energy of the sun—a village that not only sustains itself but also generates excess energy that benefits both the environment and its residents. Welcome to **Solar Village Co-Investments**—a revolutionary model of real estate that combines community living with the power of renewable energy. These solar-powered communities offer an investment opportunity that is not just financially rewarding but also part of a larger mission to create a **sustainable future**.

As we face the realities of climate change, energy independence and sustainability have become more crucial than ever. Solar Village Co-Investments aim to address these challenges by creating self-sufficient, **carbon-neutral communities** that harness the power of the sun to provide energy, economic benefits, and a new way of living. This chapter will explore how these innovative communities are transforming real estate investment into a force for positive environmental change, while offering investors a unique opportunity to be part of the renewable energy revolution.

The Vision of Solar Villages

Solar Villages are residential communities where every aspect of daily life is powered by solar energy. Imagine waking up in a house that runs entirely on renewable energy—your morning coffee brewed with solar power, your electric vehicle charged by the sun, and your home's temperature regulated by energy-efficient systems that draw their power from solar panels on your roof. These villages are designed to be **energy-independent**, generating all the electricity they need on-site and even selling excess energy back to the grid, creating an additional revenue stream for investors and residents alike.

The vision behind Solar Villages is simple: to create **sustainable, self-reliant communities** where people can live in harmony with the environment while enjoying all the conveniences of modern life. These villages are built using **eco-friendly materials**, incorporate energy-efficient designs, and feature shared amenities that encourage a sense of community and connection. The result is a living environment that is not only good for the planet but also for the people who call it home.

Investing in Renewable Energy and Community

Solar Village Co-Investments offer a unique blend of **real estate and renewable energy investment**. Investors are not just buying property—they are investing in the energy infrastructure that powers the community. Each home in a Solar Village is equipped with **solar panels**, **battery storage**, and **smart energy management systems** that optimize energy usage and ensure that the community remains energy-positive.

The excess energy generated by the village is sold back to the grid, providing a steady stream of **passive income** for investors. This revenue model makes Solar Villages an attractive investment opportunity, as it combines the stability of real estate with the growing potential of renewable energy. As the world continues to shift towards sustainable energy solutions, the value of these solar-powered communities is only expected to rise, offering investors both **financial returns** and the satisfaction of contributing to a greener future.

A Sustainable Lifestyle for Residents

Living in a Solar Village means more than just having solar panels on your roof—it's about embracing a **sustainable lifestyle**. These communities are designed to minimize their environmental footprint while maximizing the quality of life for their residents. Homes are built using **sustainable construction materials** and are designed to be highly energy-efficient, with features like natural ventilation, green roofs, and rainwater harvesting systems.

The community layout is also designed with sustainability in mind. Streets are lined with **solar-powered streetlights**, community gardens provide fresh, locally grown produce, and shared electric vehicle charging stations encourage the use of clean transportation. The emphasis on sustainability extends to every aspect of life in a Solar Village, creating an environment where residents can live comfortably while knowing that they are making a positive impact on the planet.

Imagine a neighborhood where children play in green spaces that are irrigated with harvested rainwater, where neighbors come together to tend community gardens, and where the entire community is powered by the sun. Solar Villages are not just about energy independence—they are about creating a **sense of community**, where residents work together to build a sustainable future.

Shared Amenities and Community Connection

Solar Villages are designed to foster a sense of **community and connection** among residents. The emphasis on shared amenities helps to create opportunities for interaction and collaboration. Imagine a village with a **solar-powered community center**, where residents can gather for events, workshops, and celebrations. Picture a neighborhood with **shared greenhouses** and gardens, where families can grow their own vegetables and herbs, and where gardening becomes a communal activity that brings people together.

These shared amenities are powered by the village's solar energy system, making them not only environmentally friendly but also economically efficient. By pooling resources, residents can enjoy amenities that they might not be able to afford individually—such as a **solar-heated swimming pool**, a **community workspace** with renewable energy-powered technology, or an **outdoor cinema** that runs on solar power. The result is a vibrant, connected community where people come together to share, learn, and grow.

Energy Independence and Resilience

One of the most compelling aspects of Solar Villages is their focus on **energy independence and resilience**. In a world where climate change is leading to more frequent and severe natural disasters, the ability to generate and store your own energy is becoming increasingly important. Solar Villages are designed to be **off-grid capable**, with battery storage systems that ensure a continuous power supply even during grid outages.

This resilience makes Solar Villages an attractive option for those looking to protect themselves from the uncertainties of a changing climate. Whether it's a heatwave, a storm, or a power outage, residents can rest easy knowing that their community is equipped to handle whatever comes their way. The combination of solar power and battery storage provides a level of **energy security** that is rare in traditional residential developments, making Solar Villages a model for the future of resilient living.

Economic and Environmental Impact

Solar Village Co-Investments offer a powerful way for investors to make a positive impact—both **economically and environmentally**. By investing in these communities, investors are helping to drive the adoption of renewable energy, reduce carbon emissions, and create sustainable living environments that benefit both people and the planet. The revenue generated from selling excess energy back to the grid provides a steady return on investment, while the increasing demand for sustainable housing ensures that the value of these properties will continue to grow.

In addition to the financial benefits, Solar Villages have a significant **environmental impact**. By reducing reliance on fossil fuels, these communities help to lower greenhouse gas emissions, improve air quality, and reduce the overall carbon footprint of residential living. The focus on sustainability also extends to water conservation, waste reduction, and biodiversity, making Solar Villages a comprehensive solution to some of the most pressing environmental challenges of our time.

A Model for the Future

Solar Villages are more than just a new kind of residential development—they are a **model for the future of living**. As the world grapples with the challenges of climate change, resource depletion, and population growth, there is a growing need for communities that are **sustainable, resilient, and self-sufficient**. Solar Villages provide a blueprint for how we can create neighborhoods that are not only energy-independent but also economically viable and socially connected.

Imagine a future where entire cities are composed of solar-powered communities—where every neighborhood generates its own energy, where residents work together to create sustainable solutions, and where the concept of "waste" is replaced by a focus on resource efficiency and regeneration. Solar Villages are the first step toward this future, offering a glimpse of what is possible when we combine **innovation, community, and a commitment to sustainability**.

Solar Village Co-Investments: Powering a Brighter Future

Solar Village Co-Investments represent a new way to think about real estate—one that goes beyond bricks and mortar to include **energy, sustainability, and community**. By investing in these solar-powered communities, you are not just buying property—you are investing in a vision of the future where energy is clean, communities are connected, and living is in harmony with the planet.

Whether you are an investor looking to be part of the renewable energy revolution, a family seeking a sustainable place to call home, or simply someone who believes in the power of community to create positive change, Solar Villages offer a unique opportunity to be part of something bigger. It's about more than just financial returns—it's about creating a legacy of sustainability, resilience, and innovation. Welcome to Solar Villages—where **community and sustainability** come together to power a brighter future.

Key Features: Green-powered income, shared EV infrastructure, rental and energy sales, energy independence, community-driven amenities, resilience to climate challenges.

Solar Villages are a testament to what is possible when we harness the power of renewable energy to create thriving, connected communities. They offer a new way of living—one that is sustainable, resilient, and in tune with the natural world. It's time to invest in a future where **energy independence and community connection** are at the heart of real estate. It's time to be part of the **solar-powered revolution**.

Chapter 9: Space-Shared Real Estate

The Future of Urban Living—Flexible, Adaptable, and Shared

Imagine living in a home that changes with your lifestyle—a place where you can expand, shrink, or adapt your living space based on your needs, all without the burdens of traditional ownership. Welcome to **Space-Shared Real Estate**, a revolutionary urban living concept that redefines property ownership and community living through flexibility, adaptability, and sharing. In a future where urban spaces are limited, and people crave both convenience and connection, Space-Shared Real Estate is transforming how we live, interact, and thrive in our cities.

Space-Shared Real Estate offers a vision of urban living that is **dynamic, collaborative, and sustainable**. It is a model designed for people who value freedom, who seek a sense of community, and who are willing to embrace a new way of thinking about space and ownership. This chapter explores how these innovative urban communities are reshaping the future of real estate by allowing people to live, work, and grow in spaces that adapt to their ever-changing needs.

The Concept of Space-Shared Real Estate

Space-Shared Real Estate is built on the idea that the spaces we inhabit should be as flexible and dynamic as our lives. Unlike traditional real estate, which ties residents to a fixed space, Space-Shared Real Estate allows people to **share and adapt** their living environment based on their needs. Imagine a community where you have your own private living space, but also have access to a wide array of **shared facilities and spaces** that you can use on demand—whether it's a workspace, a kitchen, a guest suite, or a yoga studio.

The concept is simple: rather than each household having all the amenities it may only use occasionally, these amenities are **centralized and shared**. Residents live in efficiently designed private units and have access to an expansive set of shared spaces, which can be booked or accessed when needed. This model not only reduces the environmental impact of redundant amenities but also fosters a sense of community and connection among residents.

Imagine being able to **expand your living space** when family visits for the holidays or downsize when you want a simpler lifestyle. Space-Shared Real Estate provides the flexibility to adapt your living environment to the rhythms of your life—ensuring that you always have the space you need without the waste or expense of unused rooms and amenities.

Flexible Living for a New Generation

Space-Shared Real Estate is designed for a new generation of urban dwellers—people who value **experiences over possessions** and who seek **flexibility over permanence**. It is perfect for those who crave the freedom to adapt their living environment as their needs change, whether that means moving to a smaller unit after downsizing, expanding into a larger space during a life transition, or simply having access to additional facilities on a temporary basis.

In a Space-Shared community, residents can **customize their living experience** by choosing from a range of shared amenities. Need a private office for a few weeks? Book one of the shared workspaces. Hosting a dinner party? Reserve the gourmet communal kitchen. Have friends visiting from out of town? Use the shared guest suite. This ability to access spaces and amenities as needed ensures that residents are always able to live comfortably without the burden of owning or maintaining spaces they seldom use.

This model is especially appealing to **digital nomads, young professionals, and retirees** who are looking for a sense of community without the long-term commitment of owning a traditional home. It allows for a level of **personalization and flexibility** that is difficult to achieve in conventional urban housing, making it ideal for those who value adaptability and want to make the most out of their living environment.

Community-Centric Design

Space-Shared Real Estate is about more than just flexible spaces—it's about building a **community**. The emphasis on shared amenities encourages interaction and collaboration, creating opportunities for residents to connect with one another in meaningful ways. Imagine a residential building with shared rooftop gardens, communal kitchens, co-working spaces, and wellness areas where residents can come together for activities, events, and shared experiences.

The **community-centric design** of these spaces fosters a sense of belonging and camaraderie among residents. The shared spaces are designed to be **beautiful, functional, and welcoming**, creating an environment where people feel comfortable and inspired to spend time. Whether it's a weekly cooking class in the shared kitchen, a yoga session in the community wellness center, or a movie night in the shared lounge, Space-Shared Real Estate creates countless opportunities for residents to come together and form lasting connections.

By integrating **social spaces** into the very fabric of the community, Space-Shared Real Estate creates a living environment that is about more than just having a place to sleep—it's about creating a home where people feel supported, connected, and engaged. This sense of community is particularly important in urban areas, where people often feel isolated despite being surrounded by others. Space-Shared Real Estate provides a solution to this challenge by creating a living environment that encourages **interaction, collaboration, and shared experiences**.

Sustainable Urban Living

Space-Shared Real Estate is also a model for **sustainable urban living**. By sharing amenities and reducing the need for every household to have its own version of every facility, these communities significantly reduce their **environmental footprint**. Shared kitchens, guest rooms, and workspaces mean fewer resources are needed to build and maintain redundant spaces, resulting in **lower energy consumption and reduced waste**.

The buildings are also designed with sustainability in mind, incorporating **energy-efficient systems, solar power**, and **green roofs** to minimize their impact on the environment. The emphasis on shared resources extends to transportation as well, with **shared electric vehicles** and bike-sharing programs that make it easy for residents to get around without the need for individual car ownership.

In addition to reducing environmental impact, the efficient use of space in these communities makes urban living more affordable. By sharing amenities, residents are able to enjoy a higher standard of living at a lower cost, making Space-Shared Real Estate an attractive option for those looking to live sustainably without sacrificing comfort or convenience.

A New Kind of Urban Flexibility

Space-Shared Real Estate introduces a level of **flexibility** that is rare in traditional urban housing. Residents can choose to expand or contract their living spaces as their needs change, without the hassle of buying, selling, or moving to a new home. This flexibility is especially valuable in a fast-paced world where careers, family situations, and personal preferences can change rapidly.

For instance, imagine a young couple moving into a Space-Shared community. They start with a small, cozy unit that meets their needs perfectly. As their family grows, they can easily expand their space by accessing additional shared units or booking extra rooms when needed. When the children move out, they can downsize again, making their living environment more manageable without having to leave the community they've come to love. This **fluid approach to living** allows people to remain in the same community throughout different stages of life, creating a sense of stability and belonging.

The Economic Benefits of Space-Shared Living

Space-Shared Real Estate is not only beneficial for residents but also offers compelling **economic advantages** for investors. By maximizing the use of shared amenities, developers can create high-quality living environments at a lower cost, while also generating additional income through the rental of shared spaces and facilities. This model ensures that the property is always being utilized to its full potential, creating a steady stream of revenue.

For investors, the appeal of Space-Shared Real Estate lies in its **resilience and adaptability**. The ability to reconfigure spaces based on demand means that these properties are always able to meet the needs of their residents, ensuring high occupancy rates and a consistent return on investment. Additionally, the focus on community and sustainability makes these properties highly attractive to a growing demographic of urban dwellers who are looking for a new way to live—one that is flexible, affordable, and environmentally responsible.

A Lifestyle of Freedom and Connection

Ultimately, Space-Shared Real Estate is about creating a **lifestyle** that offers both **freedom and connection**. It's about providing people with the flexibility to adapt their living environment to their needs while also creating opportunities for meaningful social interaction. It's a model that recognizes that our lives are not static—that our living spaces should be able to evolve as we do.

In a Space-Shared community, residents have the freedom to live life on their own terms. They can expand their living space when they need to, access high-quality amenities without the burden of ownership, and be part of a community that values **collaboration, sustainability, and connection**. It's a way of living that embraces the best of urban life—vibrancy, diversity, and opportunity—while also providing the support and connection that come from being part of a close-knit community.

Space-Shared Real Estate: The Future of Urban Living

Space-Shared Real Estate represents a new way of thinking about urban living—one that is **adaptable, sustainable, and community-focused**. By creating flexible spaces that can be shared and adapted to meet the changing needs of residents, these communities are offering a new level of convenience, connection, and quality of life. They are designed for those who want to make the most of their living environment—people who value experiences, community, and the freedom to live life on their own terms.

Whether you're a young professional looking for a vibrant community, a family in need of flexibility, or a retiree seeking a supportive environment, Space-Shared Real Estate offers a way to live that is truly in tune with the way we live today. It's about more than just having a place to live—it's about having a **home that grows, adapts, and connects**. Welcome to the future of urban living—welcome to **Space-Shared Real Estate**.

Key Features: Flexible living units, on-demand amenities, shared community spaces, sustainability, economic resilience, urban adaptability, community-driven interactions.

Space-Shared Real Estate is redefining what it means to live in a city—offering a new level of **freedom, connection, and adaptability** that meets the needs of modern urban dwellers. It's time to embrace a new way of living—one that is **flexible, collaborative, and built for the future**. Step into a community that grows with you, adapts to your needs, and brings you closer to the people around you.

Chapter 10: Gamified Living Estates

Where Real Estate Meets Adventure and Gamification

Imagine living in a neighbourhood where your daily life feels like a game—where completing everyday tasks, making new friends, and achieving personal goals earn you rewards, recognition, and a deep sense of satisfaction. Welcome to **Gamified Living Estates**—a revolutionary concept that merges real estate with the principles of **gamification**, transforming ordinary residential life into an exciting, interactive, and adventure-filled experience. In a future where entertainment, technology, and community blend seamlessly, Gamified Living Estates offer a new way to live, where **everyday activities are designed to be fun, meaningful, and engaging**.

Gamified Living Estates are designed to make life **exciting and rewarding**. They use elements like points, challenges, leaderboards, and community quests to incentivize residents to participate, engage, and grow. Imagine a place where the act of recycling earns you community points, where taking part in a neighborhood clean-up unlocks special perks, and where helping a neighbor levels you up in the community hierarchy. This chapter explores how gamification can transform the experience of living, making it both **socially rewarding and personally fulfilling**.

The Concept of Gamified Living Estates

Gamified Living Estates are residential communities where game mechanics are applied to daily life, creating an environment that is **interactive and motivating**. Imagine a world where you can earn points for fitness achievements, where completing challenges helps you unlock exclusive amenities, and where the community comes together to complete quests that benefit everyone. This unique approach to real estate encourages people to be active participants in their community, transforming everyday activities into opportunities for fun and achievement.

At the core of Gamified Living Estates is the belief that life should be both **productive and enjoyable**. These communities are designed to engage residents on multiple levels—physically, mentally, and socially—by turning mundane tasks into **exciting challenges** and meaningful competitions. The neighborhood is equipped with a **digital platform** that tracks residents' progress, rewards achievements, and encourages friendly competition. Whether it's a fitness challenge, a creative contest, or a community improvement quest, every aspect of life in a Gamified Living Estate is designed to make residents feel like they are part of a grand adventure.

Daily Life as an Adventure

In a Gamified Living Estate, everyday life is transformed into a series of **quests, challenges, and adventures**. Imagine starting your day with a fitness quest—a morning run around the neighborhood trail, where you collect virtual tokens along the way that can be redeemed for rewards like free yoga classes or a discount at the local café. Later in the day, you might take part in a community garden challenge, where residents compete to grow the healthiest vegetables, earning points that contribute to the community leaderboard.

Residents can also participate in **community-wide quests** that bring everyone together for a common goal. Imagine a weekend challenge where the entire neighborhood works together to build a new playground, with each participant earning points based on their contributions. These points can be used to unlock exclusive community perks, like access to a private rooftop lounge or a special event hosted in the community center. By gamifying community activities, residents are motivated to **get involved,** connect with their neighbors, and make their community a better place.

The gamified experience also extends to **personal growth and wellness**. Residents are encouraged to set personal goals—whether it's learning a new skill, improving their fitness, or reducing their carbon footprint—and earn rewards for their progress. Imagine receiving a badge for completing a month-long meditation challenge or for reducing your energy consumption by 20%. These achievements are celebrated within the community, creating a culture of positivity, motivation, and **continuous improvement**.

Social Connection Through Play

One of the key benefits of Gamified Living Estates is the way they foster **social connection**. By incorporating game elements into everyday life, these communities encourage residents to interact, collaborate, and form meaningful relationships. Imagine a neighborhood where making new friends is part of the game—where introducing yourself to a new neighbor earns you points, and where collaborating on a community project helps you level up in the community's social ranking system.

The use of **leaderboards and group challenges** encourages friendly competition and collaboration, bringing residents closer together. Whether it's a team-based cooking contest, a trivia night at the community center, or a scavenger hunt that takes residents on an adventure through the neighborhood, Gamified Living Estates provide countless opportunities for residents to bond over shared experiences. The result is a community that feels **vibrant, connected, and full of life**.

The gamified elements also help to **break down barriers** and make socializing easier. For people who might be shy or new to the area, the structured nature of gamified activities provides an easy way to get involved and meet others. By turning social interaction into a game, residents are encouraged to step out of their comfort zones and build lasting connections with their neighbors.

Rewarding Good Behavior and Community Contribution

Gamified Living Estates are designed to encourage **positive behavior** and active community participation. Residents are rewarded for actions that benefit both themselves and the community—whether it's recycling, conserving energy, volunteering, or helping a neighbor. These actions earn points that can be redeemed for various rewards, such as exclusive access to community amenities, discounts at local businesses, or even rent credits.

Imagine earning points every time you use the community's **composting facility** or take public transportation instead of driving. Over time, these points accumulate, allowing you to unlock special perks, such as a reserved parking spot, a free massage at the wellness center, or an invitation to an exclusive community dinner. By rewarding residents for making positive contributions, Gamified Living Estates create a culture of **mutual support and shared responsibility**.

Community contribution is also celebrated through **events and recognition ceremonies**. Residents who make significant contributions—such as leading a community project or consistently helping others—are recognized and celebrated at community gatherings. This recognition not only motivates individuals to continue contributing but also inspires others to get involved. It's about creating a community where everyone feels **valued and appreciated** for their efforts.

A Digital Platform for Engagement

The gamified experience in these estates is made possible through a **digital platform** that tracks residents' progress, displays leaderboards, and facilitates challenges and quests. Each resident has a profile on the platform, where they can set personal goals, track their achievements, and see how they compare to others in the community. The platform also serves as a hub for community communication, where residents can join challenges, sign up for events, and connect with their neighbors.

The use of **augmented reality (AR)** adds an extra layer of excitement to the gamified experience. Imagine using your smartphone to view hidden clues during a scavenger hunt or to see virtual rewards appear as you complete a challenge. The integration of AR makes the experience more immersive and engaging, turning the neighborhood into a playground where there's always something new to discover.

The digital platform also includes features for **community collaboration**, such as forums, chat groups, and event calendars. Residents can use these tools to organize their own challenges, form teams, and share their progress. The platform is designed to be intuitive and user-friendly, making it easy for residents of all ages to get involved and participate in the gamified experience.

A New Way to Experience Homeownership

Gamified Living Estates offer a new way to experience **homeownership**—one that is dynamic, interactive, and community-focused. For investors, these estates represent a unique opportunity to be part of an innovative real estate model that appeals to a growing demographic of people who value **experiences over possessions**. The gamified elements not only enhance the living experience but also create a strong sense of **community loyalty**, ensuring high occupancy rates and a stable return on investment.

The estates are designed to be **scalable**, with the gamified elements easily adaptable to different types of properties and communities. Whether it's a small apartment complex or a large residential neighbourhood, the principles of gamification can be applied to create an engaging and rewarding living environment. This scalability makes Gamified Living Estates an attractive investment opportunity, with the potential to transform residential developments around the world.

Gamified Living Estates: Where Life is a Game

Gamified Living Estates represent a bold new vision for the future of urban living—one where everyday life is transformed into an adventure, and where residents are motivated to be their best selves. By combining the principles of gamification with the stability of real estate, these communities offer a lifestyle that is both **fun and fulfilling**. It's about more than just having a place to live—it's about living in a place that inspires, motivates, and rewards you every day.

For those who want to live in a community that is **engaging, supportive, and full of life**, Gamified Living Estates offer the perfect solution. Whether you're an investor looking for a property with a unique value proposition, a young professional seeking an exciting and social environment, or a family looking for a place where everyone can thrive, these estates provide an experience like no other. Welcome to Gamified Living Estates—where **everyday life becomes an adventure**, and where the rewards are as real as the connections you make.

Key Features: Gamified community engagement, reward systems, augmented reality integration, community quests, digital platform for tracking progress, social interaction incentives, scalable living model.

Gamified Living Estates are redefining what it means to live in a residential community. They offer a new level of **interaction, motivation, and excitement** that transforms the traditional concept of homeownership into something far more **dynamic and rewarding**. Step into a community where life is a game—where every action, every connection, and every achievement is celebrated and rewarded.

Chapter 11: Quantum AI-Based Property Flip Fund

Revolutionizing Real Estate Investment Through Quantum Computing

Imagine harnessing the power of quantum computing to make precise real estate investment decisions—purchasing undervalued properties, renovating them for maximum value, and selling them at the perfect time, all with the analytical capability of an advanced AI system. Welcome to the **Quantum AI-Based Property Flip Fund**, a cutting-edge concept that combines quantum computing and artificial intelligence to revolutionize property flipping. This chapter explores how the integration of quantum computing with real estate creates a new frontier of profitability, efficiency, and innovation.

The Quantum AI-Based Property Flip Fund is about **using technology to eliminate guesswork** from property investment. With quantum computing's unmatched processing power and AI's ability to learn and adapt, this fund is capable of analyzing an incredible amount of data—from market trends and local demographics to economic indicators and renovation costs—in real-time. It's about flipping properties with a level of insight and accuracy that human investors simply cannot achieve, resulting in **optimized profits and minimized risks**.

The Concept of Quantum AI in Real Estate

The **Quantum AI-Based Property Flip Fund** uses quantum computing to process complex datasets that traditional computers struggle with. Quantum computers operate at speeds exponentially faster than classical computers, allowing them to solve problems and run simulations that would take ordinary machines years to complete. By leveraging this technology, the fund can analyze **massive amounts of data** to identify the best investment opportunities and predict market changes with greater accuracy.

Imagine being able to pinpoint the perfect neighborhood to invest in before it becomes popular, or identifying the ideal moment to sell a property based on future price predictions. The Quantum AI system can evaluate millions of potential scenarios, calculate risk factors, and provide data-driven recommendations for each investment. This level of precision ensures that properties are purchased at the lowest possible cost, renovated for maximum value, and sold at the most opportune time—**maximizing returns for investors**.

Quantum Computing Meets AI: A Perfect Match

The **combination of quantum computing and AI** is what makes this property flip fund truly revolutionary. Quantum computing's ability to process complex variables is paired with AI's machine learning algorithms, which can learn from historical data and adapt to changing market conditions. The AI continuously learns from each property flip, refining its strategies to improve future performance.

For example, the AI system can learn which types of renovations provide the highest return on investment in specific markets, which neighborhoods are likely to see increased demand, and how economic factors like interest rates or unemployment levels impact property values. By integrating these insights with the processing power of quantum computing, the fund is able to make **smarter, faster, and more informed decisions** than any human investor or traditional investment fund.

The Quantum AI analyzes factors such as **property conditions, renovation costs, market trends, buyer preferences, and even**

local regulations. It considers everything from nearby schools and crime rates to the historical appreciation of similar properties, providing a level of analysis that is incredibly comprehensive. This allows the fund to not only identify undervalued properties but also to create a **tailored renovation plan** that maximizes the property's market value.

Data-Driven Property Selection and Flipping

The process begins with the AI analyzing a vast array of **property listings**, identifying those that have the potential for significant appreciation. These properties might be undervalued due to neglect, market conditions, or simply being overlooked by traditional investors. The AI can identify hidden gems—properties that others may miss—by analyzing patterns that are not apparent to the human eye.

Once a property is selected, the AI designs a **renovation strategy** that maximizes return on investment. It calculates which improvements are most likely to increase the property's value, whether it's upgrading the kitchen, adding energy-efficient features, or enhancing curb appeal. The AI can even suggest materials and suppliers, optimizing renovation costs to ensure that the project stays within budget while delivering maximum impact.

When it comes to **selling the property**, the Quantum AI determines the optimal timing by analyzing current market conditions, future projections, and buyer behavior patterns. It might recommend holding the property for a few extra months to take advantage of an expected market upswing, or selling quickly if indicators suggest a downturn. This level of **strategic decision-making** ensures that each property flip yields the highest possible profit.

Minimizing Risks with Predictive Analysis

One of the key benefits of the Quantum AI-Based Property Flip Fund is its ability to **minimize risks** through predictive analysis. Traditional property flipping involves a certain level of risk—unexpected renovation costs, changes in market conditions, or delays in selling can all impact profitability. By using quantum computing to analyze data and run simulations, the fund can predict potential risks and develop strategies to mitigate them.

For example, the AI can predict potential **supply chain disruptions** that could delay renovation projects and suggest alternatives in advance. It can also identify potential regulatory changes that could impact property values, allowing the fund to make proactive decisions. By anticipating challenges before they arise, the Quantum AI-Based Property Flip Fund is able to reduce the risks associated with property flipping and ensure more consistent returns for investors.

A New Level of Transparency and Efficiency

The use of **blockchain technology** adds an additional layer of transparency and security to the Quantum AI-Based Property Flip Fund. All transactions, from property purchases to renovation costs and sales, are recorded on a blockchain, providing a clear and immutable record of each step in the investment process. This transparency is particularly appealing to investors, who can track their investments in real-time and have confidence in the integrity of the fund's operations.

The integration of blockchain also enhances **efficiency** by automating various aspects of the investment process. Smart contracts can be used to execute transactions automatically when certain conditions are met, reducing the need for intermediaries and minimizing transaction costs. For example, a smart contract could automatically release funds to a contractor once a renovation milestone is completed, ensuring that projects stay on schedule and within budget.

High Returns and Scalable Investment Opportunities

The Quantum AI-Based Property Flip Fund is designed to deliver **high returns** by using technology to optimize every aspect of the property flipping process. The combination of quantum computing's predictive power and AI's adaptive learning ensures that each investment decision is backed by data and driven by insight. This approach not only maximizes profitability but also reduces the risks that often come with property flipping.

The fund is also highly **scalable**, making it possible to manage multiple property flips simultaneously across different markets. Quantum computing's processing power allows the fund to analyze and manage a large number of properties at once, making it possible to expand operations without sacrificing accuracy or efficiency. This scalability means that the Quantum AI-Based Property Flip Fund has the potential to become a major player in the real estate market, offering **attractive returns for investors** while transforming how properties are bought, renovated, and sold.

Quantum AI-Based Property Flip Fund: The Future of Real Estate Investment

The Quantum AI-Based Property Flip Fund represents the future of real estate investment—where technology takes center stage, transforming how we identify, purchase, and profit from properties. By leveraging the power of quantum computing and AI, this fund is able to make **data-driven decisions** that maximize returns, minimize risks, and create a more efficient and transparent investment process.

Whether you're an experienced investor looking for high returns, a tech enthusiast interested in the potential of quantum computing, or someone who wants to be part of an innovative investment opportunity, the Quantum AI-Based Property Flip Fund offers a solution that is both **cutting-edge and highly profitable**. It's about using the latest technology to take the guesswork out of property flipping and create a smarter, more efficient way to invest in real estate.

Welcome to the future of property investment—welcome to **Quantum AI-Based Property Flip Fund**, where **technology meets real estate** to create unparalleled opportunities for growth and profitability.

Key Features: Quantum computing for data analysis, AI-driven property selection and renovation, risk minimization through predictive analysis, blockchain-based transparency, smart contract automation, scalable flipping operations.

The Quantum AI-Based Property Flip Fund is redefining property investment by integrating the power of **quantum computing, AI, and blockchain**. It's time to embrace a new way of flipping properties—one that is smarter, faster, and more profitable than ever before. Step into the world of Quantum AI-Based Property Flip Fund and experience the **future of real estate** today.

Chapter 12: Impact Pods for Regenerative Living

Sustainable Communities Designed to Regenerate the Planet

Imagine living in a community that not only reduces its environmental footprint but actively works to regenerate the land and restore the balance of the ecosystem—where every home, garden, and shared space is designed with the health of the planet in mind. Welcome to **Impact Pods for Regenerative Living**, a visionary real estate model that aims to create communities that are in harmony with nature, where residents contribute to restoring biodiversity, enhancing soil health, and improving the local environment. This chapter explores how Impact Pods are setting a new standard for sustainable living by making regeneration the central focus of residential development.

Impact Pods for Regenerative Living are designed to be **self-sustaining, eco-friendly communities** that give more back to the environment than they take. Picture living in a home that generates its own energy, produces its own food, and is part of a broader network of similar homes working together to create a thriving, regenerative ecosystem. These communities are about more than just sustainability—they are about **actively improving** the world around them.

The Concept of Regenerative Living

Regenerative living goes beyond the idea of minimizing harm to the environment. It's about creating systems that actively work to regenerate and restore the natural environment. Impact Pods are built on this principle, incorporating regenerative agriculture, renewable energy, and green building practices to create communities that are not only **carbon-neutral** but also work to restore the land and enhance biodiversity.

Each Impact Pod is a **modular, eco-friendly home** that is designed to blend seamlessly with the natural landscape. The homes are built using sustainable materials and incorporate features like **green roofs, rainwater harvesting systems, and solar panels**. The community as a whole is designed to function as an interconnected ecosystem, with each Pod contributing to the overall health and vitality of the environment.

Imagine a village of Impact Pods nestled in a lush landscape, where gardens and green spaces are designed to attract pollinators, soil health is enhanced through composting and regenerative practices, and every aspect of the community is optimized to promote **biodiversity and environmental health**. It's a model of living that not only sustains the residents but also sustains the planet.

Self-Sustaining and Renewable

Impact Pods are designed to be **self-sustaining**, with each home generating its own energy and producing its own food. Solar panels, wind turbines, and geothermal systems provide **renewable energy**, ensuring that the community is not reliant on fossil fuels. Energy storage systems are integrated into each Pod, allowing residents to store surplus energy for use during cloudy or windless days.

Food production is also an essential aspect of Impact Pods. Each Pod is equipped with **vertical gardens, hydroponic systems, and edible landscaping** that allow residents to grow their own fruits, vegetables, and herbs. Community gardens and orchards provide additional food resources, creating a local, resilient food system that reduces the community's carbon footprint and enhances food security. By producing their own food, residents are able to **reduce waste, eliminate food miles**, and enjoy fresh, organic produce year-round.

Water is another key resource that is managed sustainably within Impact Pods. **Rainwater harvesting systems** collect and store water for household and garden use, while greywater recycling systems ensure that no drop is wasted. These systems are designed to work in harmony with the natural environment, providing clean, fresh water without depleting local resources.

A Community of Regenerative Stewards

Impact Pods are more than just homes—they are part of a community of people who are committed to **regenerating the planet**. The emphasis on community is central to the concept of regenerative living, with residents working together to create a thriving ecosystem that supports both people and the planet. Imagine a village where neighbors come together to tend community gardens, restore local habitats, and support each other in living sustainably.

The community is designed to be **collaborative and inclusive**, with shared spaces like community kitchens, workshops, and event areas where residents can come together to share skills, resources, and knowledge. Regular workshops and events are held to teach residents about regenerative practices, from composting and permaculture to wildlife conservation and renewable energy systems. The goal is to create a culture of **learning, sharing, and collective action**, where everyone is empowered to contribute to the regeneration of the land.

Residents are also encouraged to be **stewards of the environment**. Each Pod is equipped with sensors that monitor energy use, water consumption, and environmental conditions, providing residents with real-time data that helps them make informed decisions about their resource use. By providing residents with the tools and knowledge they need to live regeneratively, Impact Pods are creating a new generation of environmental stewards who are committed to making a positive impact on the planet.

Restoring Biodiversity and Ecosystem Health

A key goal of Impact Pods for Regenerative Living is to **restore biodiversity** and improve ecosystem health. The communities are designed to be wildlife-friendly, with green spaces that provide habitats for birds, insects, and other animals. **Native plants** are used in landscaping to attract pollinators and provide food and shelter for local wildlife, while ponds and wetlands create habitats for amphibians and aquatic species.

Imagine walking through your community and seeing butterflies and bees buzzing among wildflowers, birds nesting in native trees, and frogs hopping around a community pond. These vibrant, biodiverse environments are not just beautiful—they are essential for the health of the planet. By creating habitats that support a wide range of species, Impact Pods are helping to **restore the balance of local ecosystems** and promote biodiversity.

The emphasis on regenerative agriculture also plays a key role in restoring ecosystem health. Community gardens are managed using **regenerative farming practices** that improve soil health, sequester carbon, and promote biodiversity. By avoiding the use of chemical pesticides and fertilizers, these gardens create a safe, healthy environment for both people and wildlife. The result is a community that is not only self-sustaining but also works to **heal the land** and restore the natural environment.

A New Model for Sustainable Development

Impact Pods for Regenerative Living represent a new model for **sustainable development**—one that goes beyond reducing harm to actively creating positive impacts. Traditional sustainable development focuses on minimizing the negative effects of human activity, but regenerative development aims to **restore, renew, and revitalize** the natural environment. Impact Pods are designed to achieve this by integrating regenerative principles into every aspect of community life, from energy and food production to water management and community engagement.

This model is not only beneficial for the environment—it also creates a **resilient and thriving community**. By producing their own food, generating their own energy, and managing their own water resources, Impact Pods are less vulnerable to external disruptions, such as supply chain issues or energy shortages. The emphasis on community and collaboration also creates a strong social network, providing residents with the support they need to thrive.

Impact Pods: A Vision for the Future

Impact Pods for Regenerative Living offer a **vision for the future**—a future where communities are designed to work in harmony with the natural world, where residents are active participants in regenerating the environment, and where the focus is on creating a positive impact rather than simply minimizing harm. By integrating regenerative principles into every aspect of community life, Impact Pods are setting a new standard for sustainable living—one that is **holistic, inclusive, and future-focused**.

Whether you're looking for a place to call home, an opportunity to be part of a regenerative movement, or an investment in the future of sustainable development, Impact Pods offer a solution that is both innovative and impactful. It's about creating a place where people can live in harmony with nature, where every action contributes to the health of the planet, and where communities thrive by giving back more than they take.

Welcome to Impact Pods for Regenerative Living—where **sustainability meets regeneration**, and where the future of real estate is about **healing the planet** and creating thriving, resilient communities.

Key Features: Modular eco-friendly homes, renewable energy systems, regenerative agriculture, collaborative community spaces, biodiversity restoration, real-time resource monitoring, resilience through self-sufficiency.

Impact Pods for Regenerative Living are redefining what it means to live sustainably. They offer a future where communities are **self-sustaining, resilient, and regenerative**—where people live not just sustainably, but in a way that actively works to **restore and enhance the environment**. It's time to embrace a new way of living—one that is **regenerative, connected, and deeply rooted in the health of the planet**.

Final Summary: A Vision for the Future of Real Estate

The journey through this book has taken us to the forefront of **real estate innovation**, exploring ideas that are reshaping how we live, invest, and interact with our environment. Each chapter has offered a glimpse into the future—one where traditional barriers are dismantled, and new opportunities arise, enabling a more inclusive, sustainable, and engaging experience in property ownership and living.

From **Fractional Investment Models** and **Digital Nomad Co-Living Spaces** to the forward-thinking **Quantum AI-Based Property Flip Fund** and **Impact Pods for Regenerative Living**, this book has highlighted how technology, sustainability, and community are converging to redefine the real estate landscape. The concepts presented are about more than just owning property—they are about embracing a **new mindset** that values **flexibility, accessibility, environmental stewardship, and shared experiences**.

Key Takeaways from Each Model

1. **Fractional Investment Models** allow anyone to invest in high-value real estate without the large capital requirements, democratizing access to property ownership.
2. **Digital Nomad Co-Living Spaces** cater to the growing community of remote workers, offering them vibrant, connected living environments that foster productivity and creativity.
3. **Sustainable Vertical Neighborhoods** provide an innovative response to urban density, blending nature with architecture to create greener, healthier cities.

4. **Regenerative Impact Pods** are setting new standards for living sustainably, where communities actively contribute to restoring biodiversity and enhancing local ecosystems.
5. **Quantum AI-Based Property Flip Fund** leverages the cutting-edge power of quantum computing and AI to optimize property investments, maximizing returns and minimizing risks.
6. **Cloud-Connected Villages** merge rural tranquility with modern technology, offering a connected living experience that enhances both community engagement and resource efficiency.
7. **Flexi-Stay Crowd-Investment Property Hub** combines the best aspects of property ownership, travel, and shared use—providing investors with flexible, global access to a network of luxury properties, along with passive income benefits.
8. **Gamified Living Estates** transform community engagement into an interactive experience, incentivizing social connections and making day-to-day life more enjoyable through rewards and challenges.

A New Era of Living, Investing, and Community Building

The future of real estate is about more than just **brick and mortar**; it is about creating **experiences**. Each concept in this book focuses on transforming real estate into a dynamic, interactive, and regenerative space that caters to the needs of the next generation. Whether it's providing **affordable access** to high-value investments, creating **engaging environments** where residents feel truly connected, or using **technology to enhance sustainability** and efficiency, these models all have one thing in common—they put people and the planet at the center of real estate innovation.

As we look towards 2030 and beyond, it's clear that **sustainability, flexibility, and community** will be the driving forces behind real estate development. The days of static, uninspired property ownership are numbered. In their place, we are seeing the rise of **regenerative, interactive, and inclusive living spaces** that empower individuals to **live well, invest smartly, and make a positive impact** on the world.

The real estate revolution is here, and it is driven by bold ideas, technological advancements, and a commitment to creating a better world for all. This book is an invitation to be part of that revolution—to rethink what real estate can be, to embrace the potential of **new technologies and innovative models**, and to imagine a future where everyone has the opportunity to thrive in spaces that are as **vibrant, diverse, and dynamic** as the people who inhabit them.

Thank you for joining this journey into the future of real estate. The time to innovate is now, and the opportunities are endless. Whether you're an investor, a developer, or someone who simply dreams of a better way to live, this book has shown that the possibilities are only limited by our imagination.

Welcome to the future of living, investing, and community building—a future where **everyone has a place, a purpose, and a voice** in shaping the spaces we call home.

www.ingramcontent.com/pod-product-compliance
Lightning Source LLC
Chambersburg PA
CBHW071106240526
45469CB00006BD/2346